Attitude!

FOR YOUR BEST LIVED LIFE

KAREN OKULICZ

K-Slaw, Inc.
P.O. Box 375
Belmar, NJ 07719
www.OKULICZ.com

Published by K-Slaw, Inc
                P.O. Box 375
                Belmar, New Jersey 07719
                (888) 529-6090

Library of Congress Control Number: 2005910418

ISBN: 978-0-9644260-2-3

First printing, January, 2006
Second printing, March, 2006
Third printing, October, 2006
Fourth printing, September, 2007

Printed in the United States of America

To my brother

Paul Neal Okulicz

The best Dad

"People are just as happy as they make up their minds to be"

Abraham Lincoln

Table of Contents

Introduction

Attitude! is the one thing that we can control and maintain to live our best life. Is this easy? Never. In this third book of mine we will gather the tools on how to recognize the joy robbers, step out of the way of the energy drainers, choose our view, care for ourselves and be good to get good.

This book was my hardest to complete as my normally good attitude was tested during the process. I have to thank those who tested me, for this book would not have made me dig deeper to find and keep my best

Attitude!

1

Attitude is Everything

Our attitude is the single most controllable aspect of ourselves. It will create our own personal heaven, or hell, on earth. Our choice of attitude determines how we process what the world hands us, and is the key to all our successes or miseries.

The purpose of this book is to assist in keeping ourselves on the best road, going forward with tools and techniques to maintain a positive attitude. We will learn to choose our view, deal with joy robbers, take the best care of ourselves and we will practice for the fun of it.

How is our attitude controllable? The definition of attitude from Webster's dictionary is: Attitude 1. A bodily posture showing mood, action etc. 2. A manner showing one's feelings or thoughts 3. One's disposition, opinion etc.

If attitude is showing one's feelings and thoughts, and feelings and thoughts are controllable, then attitude is one of the things we can control. We cannot control the weather, another person's attitude, a lay-off, late trains, missing files, unexpected health issues or accidents. What we can control is the way we **choose** to face the day's obstacles.

Whatever the situation, we control our reaction to that situation. We can live our lives blaming outside influences, and maybe have a "poor me" attitude for awhile, even hide under the covers with drama. However, our lives will arrive at a place in time when we will recognize, it is all our choice.

To say the world spins right all the time if you have a great attitude, reflects a Pollyanna way of thinking. The world is constantly changing and lots of things happen. We will have moments to years of great times, or moments to years of challenging times. It is our choice how we live in those moments or those years.

Some of the challenges we can walk around, and others we must face head on. The day we are facing might be filled with an event that is immobilizing. It will be our choice of attitude that will provide us with the best options to go forward through the day.

The best thing about attitude is that it has an equal playing field. No matter how tall or small, young or old, rich or poor we are, we all choose our attitude daily. What attitude we choose is the key to the life we live.

A life with a great attitude lived daily, goes into a life lived well for a week, a month or for a lifetime.

If attitude is always your choice, free and controllable, why not choose the best for yourself?

Here's how.

2

Joy Robber

One of the enemies of having a great attitude is the presence of a joy robber. What is a joy robber? Joy robbers are the people for whom it seems the sole purpose of their lives is to create grief for others.

The most important thing to remember is that joy robbers are everywhere, and always will be. They may come in the form of a boss, a neighbor, a relative, a new acquaintance, a stranger in the grocery store or behind a customer service counter. They are the people that bother you. Believe me, you have met them! You may have called them the rotten apple, or worse!

Joy robbers are sent to us to test our good nature with keeping a great attitude. They have the ability to drain you of your own self-love and discipline. Discipline? Yup! If you allow yourself to get caught up in their bad behavior, it keeps you off track. You need your attention focused on your own projects, your daily work or even your own fun. Joy robbers are deadly to success, if you allow them to bother you.

Now why would someone be like this? Why would someone sabotage us in the work place, create ill will in the family or at our place of worship? I believe their behavior stems from their own unhappiness and disappointment in their own lives. People who are not well, also tend to act out and try to rob your joy. Their view of the world, without joy, is not your problem.

Funny thing: when you get rid of that awful boss (a joy robber) who has been so unkind to you and upset you for days on end at your work, you are relieved. Then arrives the new relative who starts something upsetting. Why is that? I think really it is to just show us that there always will be joy robbers. No matter how long we live, we will always have them in our lives in some form. It is up to us to recognize the joy robber ("JR") and not to allow them to trap us in their ugly web.

I have worked in many offices, and with many different supervisors. Early on, I realized that no matter how often I changed my work, or it was changed for me, the same people were employed there. Not the same people, but similar types. It was like someone had taken the head of one person and put the same head on another. A different-looking person but with similar bad or great behavior.

I am sure you do this with friends or old co-workers you call them up from a new position, and they ask you how the new place is, and how the people are. You then say, "Oh, we have our 'Joe' here, or remember 'Sally'? We have one of those."

If you recognize the new "JR" at the new office, you know what you are dealing with. Having the experience from your last position, you are better equipped with how to proceed in the new position.

I would like to add that joy robbers are usually crazy. Why would a happy and centered person want to cause anyone a moment of unhappiness? They would have to be crazy. And so they are. If for no reason someone at work starts to sabotage your work, or you hear family gossip that is just so hurtful that was said about you, look at the source. No, it is not you, it is them.

What you must remember here is YOU CANNOT OUT-THINK CRAZY. Repeat after me: YOU CANNOT OUT-THINK CRAZY. If someone is starting to act in a crazy way without reason toward you, RUN. If it gets to a point where their behavior can hurt your family, your home, pets or yourself, get authorities involved. Best to file the behavior with the police, get a lawyer, go to Human Resources. Call anonymously if you feel more comfortable, whatever is needed. It is always worth it to handle them in a professional manner, both for your safety and good night's sleep.

Since YOU CANNOT OUT-THINK CRAZY, it is best not to go toe-to-toe with them. You will never win. They live in crazyland, where nothing makes sense. If you fix what they want fixed, they will focus on another thing. Remember, nothing you do will make them happy.

One of the best pieces of advice I have ever been given by a friend was when dealing with a person in "crazyland." She advised me not to wear "crazy shoes." I asked her what does that mean? She said whatever the behavior of this person is, do not get pulled into having the same behavior. Also, do not act the way they make you feel.

Wouldn't you just want to scream at that awful boss in a room full of people, "You are a bully (or worse).

No one likes you." You'll most likely lose your job, and the behavior will make you look crazy and out of control. Wouldn't you love to paint a sign on your door that says, "Stay away all joy robbers and you know who you are"? Crazy behavior. It drains you and demeans you.

We may even wish these people bad, for the agony they may have caused, but that is not the best way to get yourself any resolution. This again is that "crazy shoe" thinking. They will always have a pair of "crazy shoes" waiting. Don't even check for your size.

There are levels of joy robbers. Some we see daily, others occasionally. Arming ourselves against these people is taking care of ourselves. I am a believer that all things happen for a reason. Some reasons we know in time, and others (believe me) I will ask "Why did that happen?" at the end of my time. If all things have a rhyme and reason, why has this joy robber appeared in my life at this time? What have they to teach us?

Joy robbers may serve to direct us to move, to look for new work, put up a better fence for privacy or plan our holidays in China. Look for what the reason might be. They really do push our buttons, to find a better way of life. A better way of processing our world. If you need assistance legally, psychologically, or even spiritually to handle a joy robber, do yourself the favor and get the assistance.

After putting the situation in the authorities hands or not, a good thing to do is to just ignore them. Focus on yourself. Proceed forward to the next new job, or new place of residence or new adventure in your life. To enter into crazyland with any bad behavior on your part, makes them the winner. And we know these people are never winners. You are the winner when you handle issues with dignity and respect for yourself.

There is also the event when you run into a certain person who I'll call an energy drainer. This is harder. I always have the best intentions to stop and speak to the person. I will stop to say hello. The third degree starts. "So, how's your business?" Mind you, this is my business, not their business. I say, "Fine." Then they start with the questions, "How many books did you sell last year?" "Why haven't you been on Oprah?" I am looking around me; why did I even stop to chat? By the end of the conversation, I am drained and dragging. What happened? This type of person will drain your energy.

I don't play tennis, but when I meet this kind of character I feel like I have to have a racket in hand to lob the ball away from me. Insulting comment, hit the ball, probing question, hit the ball, sly remark, hit the ball, more probing questions, hit the ball. Exhausting for sure. Just limit the time. Look at your watch and say, "Have to go!" You may have to improvise, to just get out of the way of an energy drainer.

Once we recognize that there are, and always will be joy robbers and energy drainers in the world, it is our responsibility to gather the tools to handle them in a way that they do not harm our good nature. With these tools we will process whatever the situation is. They will not rob us of one moment of our joy or good attitude. Is it this easy? NEVER.

3

Choose your view

How we view our world obviously has a lot to do with our attitude. We have all heard the old saying, "Do you see the glass as half-empty or half-full?" A way of looking at life as an optimist or a pessimist. Which do you choose? To look at life as the glass half-empty (negatively) or half-full (positively)?

Moment to moment we choose the way we view our life. Mental views are similar to external views. We all have our favorite view of things or places. It could be a view of the ocean, or a mountain range, or a moonlit skyline. It would be wonderful if we had those views we choose all the time, but we don't. However, we can still choose our views to keep us calm, centered and balanced.

I have clever friends who live in a very crowded area in the summer. What they do is adjust their window shades in such a way that they see just the trees, and not the crowds on the sidewalk. This act makes them feel less invaded by the crowds. They do not anguish watching the trees, as they do when they are watching the throngs of summer visitors parade by their home. Maybe we all have to adjust our shades, so our views are less invasive and less annoying to us.

If you can't change the situation, can you alter the perception? Now look around you. At work could you put a picture of that ocean view/mountain view on your desk? This view of your world will assist you to keep your attitude positive, at least a little.

This choice of view, and chosen perception, also works with any social function you must attend. Do you choose to internally obsess about things you cannot change? If you go every year to the same family picnic and the same Cousin/Aunt or Uncle asks you again the same pointed questions: "When are you getting married?" or "When are you getting a divorce?" "How is that new business idea working?" (Which you made the mistake of telling them you had this business idea in the first place.) Even the silliest of "Oh, you cut your hair. I liked it long." Following year, "Oh, you grew your hair! I liked it short." These statements all from the same person. Go figure!

After a couple of times of falling into the trap of feeling bad about the said situation, "Why are you not married yet or why didn't you leave him/her yet?" "Why didn't the business work out?" Or the hair thing. Maybe you should expect the question and have an answer ready? Maybe choose a simple response. Smile; say, "Not yet." And add, "Let's eat."

Change your view of the day. You already know what will happen. Change your attitude. You'll have a much better time.

There will always be people who step over their boundaries to test your faith and patience. These aren't the joy robbers, these are the attitude testers. This type of person is sent to deflate your balloon and send you running for a tooth guard to stop you from gritting your teeth while you're in their presence.

Most of these people you know already. If you allow them to test your good attitude, when you know how they are, then this is your problem, not theirs. You cannot control them. We know this. You can only control your reaction or view of them. So, either you change the entire situation, which may not be possible at the moment, or you change your perception or view of it. Keeping you in the best attitude is of paramount importance.

Let's do a little detective work here. Are you finding attitude testers around every corner? Look closer. What is the common denominator in the situation? If you are struggling with others, look at the pattern of why things are not falling into place, and see what is the common denominator. The common denominator is usually you.

If you start listing what is wrong in your life: work never works out, love does not last, promotions pass you by, and money is always lacking. Just a list of negatives. Look closer. Who is in the center of all these issues? What is the common denominator? Is it you?

If work is not working, maybe you need to figure out what it is you would like to do. Do I hear the cry, "Oh, that takes too long." "Oh, I don't have the time." You don't have the time to have one bad day. Are you not going to school to better yourself for the next position? Or would you rather complain? Love life not working? Are you choosing unwisely? Are you wishing to marry and have a committed relationship, but spend time with unavailable partners?

Take a day, or a couple of days, and listen to your complaints. Maybe even write them down. Are they valid complaints? Can you change what you complain about? If so, stop complaining. Your time is too precious. Stop wasting it with complaining.

Since we have choice with our thoughts, what do we choose? Do I choose, on a fabulous sunny perfect day, to be angry over something or someone I cannot control? I have. What a waste of our very special limited lifetime. I am learning. We choose our internal views. Look closely. Is this you? Do you need to change your view of the situation?

Here I would like to add the choice and view of worry. What an attitude drain this is! If you choose to worry about that skin rash, the debt, the marriage, relationship, the children, parents, yourself, what does worry give you? Sleepless nights? Tiresome days? A headache, a stomachache or worse? We all do this at times. We stay in the worry and dread, which is sometimes so much our own learned patterns that when one worry clears up, we fill the space with a new worry.

We can choose to face the worry, and make that Dr.'s appointment or book a time with a marriage counselor with or without your spouse. Figure how to handle your debt. What do you need to do for your parents, your children, your welfare?

It takes courage to face worry. The challenge of facing worry is life- long. We come to realize once we face the worry, it dims. The situation is handled. We have conquered another of life's many obstacles. Easy? NEVER.

Looking at your life full, will make it full. Does this thought, action, desire, emotion serve me, or delete from me? Does this hurt me? Does this heal me? You choose your view. If I am doing things, or having thoughts that hurt me, what is the answer? Stop what hurts you. Simple? Again, NEVER.

There are many practices from stress management, to living in the moment, to prayer, to mental skills that will assist you with those internal patterns. If you need additional help with your mental patterns, seek out books, tapes, a therapist, a priest, meditation, whatever it is that will help you be your best. Gather the tools to live your best full life.

What bothers you in your view, is not necessarily a problem in someone else's view. It is also best to have a core of friends or associates with whom to share. Usually you'll get some clear direction on how to handle the said situation. "Oh, my work is so terrible, how I cannot find love, I have an issue that plagues me with my family, my spouse, my boss, what is your view on this?" You will get a different view that will assist you with the situation. You can then choose to add their view to yours. It's helpful to talk things out with trusted friends, great parents, a therapist or pets.

Sometimes by stepping outside your current situation, things become clearer. The present situation changes for you. You start looking for new work, something happens to that awful boss, you take a job somewhere else and you get promoted. WOW, a new attitude.

The choice of having a bad attitude snowballs. There is also a snowball-effect to a great attitude. If you choose to be angry with a chip on your shoulder, the world will treat you this way, and vice versa. More on cause and effect later.

Since attitude is our choice, and we can choose our view of the world moment to moment, what do we choose? Why be angry? Why be mad? Why be struggling, unhappy or disappointed? There will always be times, and people, that do make us mad and angry, leading to times of unhappiness and sadness. It is our choice of how long we sit in "it." Does it serve me, or delete from me? How long do you choose to sit in this emotion of anger, madness, etc? Your choice!

Your view is always your choice.

4

Joy

Recently, someone asked me, "How does one find joy?" What a great question! I thought about this, then answered, "From what I see in others, there is a direct correlation of being joyful with being grateful or thankful."

The person looked at me as if I had two heads. "What do you mean?" he said. He then went on to ask, how could he be grateful or thankful, he had so much going on in his life. I had to think: could this be again the view of the glass half-empty or half-full? His perception of his life?

I went ahead and said, "Gratefulness is a building process. If you start your day looking at all the responsibilities you have, and all the things that could go wrong and do go wrong, how could you ever feel joy? How could one want to lift one's head from the pillow to even start a new day? Let alone keep a good attitude?"

Remember, whatever we focus on wins. If you look at what is positive, and not dwell on the negative, guess what wins? The positive every time.

Keep a gratitude journal to be reminded of all the joys in your life. This is similar to counting your blessings, but you're actually writing them down. You can also use this technique to keep your demons at bay. You write down five things you are grateful for, thus focusing on the positive. Many experts agree this is one way to keep a positive mode and promote more joy. It is usually done at the end of the day.

There are so many types of journaling to keep one's emotions in check. End of the day writing, evening, morning or midday. Just do it, as an added tool to keeping your great attitude. You choose the time that is best for you and write away. Write away the worry, the sadness, the letters of forgiveness to the living or the dead. Write down the future dreams, and the actions necessary to fill those dreams. Write what joy is in your life.

Taking pen to the paper with the gratitude journal is very calming. I have done this at various times. I am really not good at doing this daily, but in times of strife I do use this tool a lot. What can I be grateful for at this time, while I am in this or that (perceived) pickle? Again, one's pickle situation is another's day on the beach.

Remember, all emotions are always at our beck and call. Let's see, today I will pull up a seething mind and grinding teeth. I choose to be nasty and aggravated. Not the best choices, but sometimes outside factors add to the many levels of being. If you choose to see the day as so hard, so mean, so difficult, then you start the day with a knot in your stomach or start that headache on the horizon. Or you can break it down.

I am grateful for the work I do until I find the better work for myself. I am grateful for the car that takes me to the work I do, until I find the better job that will get me the better car. If I choose to have one. I am grateful for the nasty co-workers, for they may be the messengers that are there to tell me it is time for a change. Well, maybe?

Let's look at this closer. If your mind is spending time being grateful, you are armed against being unhappy and the whole mix of ugly emotions of being nasty, abusive to yourself and others. Looking at the good for a moment, then 5 minutes, then 10 minutes, go through your list in your life.

I am grateful in my health for....

I am grateful for the relationships of....

I am grateful in work for....

I am grateful in family for....

I am grateful with....

I am grateful for ....

I am grateful to ....

I am grateful ....

You *build* a life, not *have* a life.

Sometimes life will push you into being grateful for the simplest of things. What once was, may not exist anymore. This may be a time of a job lay-off, divorce, a personal illness or tragedy, or any change that disrupts the flow of your life. A change that takes away what was the normal, and now doesn't exist anymore (or for a while) can force you to focus on the simpler, more basic aspects of your life.

One year I traveled a little too much for me. So I decided to cut my travel time, to build my life in a more personally suitable way.

So, I began the next year with less travel. I was so happy to return from a work trip to a couple months working on my home turf. That very first week of being home, I fell. I fell down my cellar steps. It was just the last three steps, but enough to tear the ligaments in my left leg. I was down for the count. Weeks on the couch, months of rehab with physical therapy. I had a cane for a short time. I had no exercise of any kind for six months. I just could not stand up for any lengthy period of time.

I had to look at what I was grateful for. I was, and am, so grateful for the close friends who looked in on me. I was thrilled the first time I could stand at the sink to wash dishes. What was not a favorite chore before, became a joy to do! Because I could do it. I could stand up with weight on my leg.

I was grateful when I could take out my own garbage. OK, so these tasks are not the day in sun and fun, but they are what make a life. Our daily living is what makes us who we are. Our reactions to our daily life are what keep the joy in our lives. This is not about money, or things, this is about inner peace. Peace, you see, is a by-product of joy.

When you are doing things you like, you create your joy. Find the time to do something you like. If you are not doing this, why aren't you? This is the real test of self-worth. Why do we not find time to do what makes us happy? Are we too busy, or do we feel we do not deserve to give to ourselves? Remember, in all airplane pre-flight emergency drills we have been told put the oxygen mask on first, before we help anyone else. That means partners, children, and parents. We cannot give, unless we are giving to ourselves first. This goes for lack of cabin pressure, or daily life.

Get some adventure in your life! It will promote joy. If you don't really want the adventure, read the catalog. Volunteer at something, it will promote joy.

Baby-sitting a dog, a neighbor, a child, will give you joy. Sometimes simply showing up is enough to create joy, in yourself as well as the person(s) you showed up for. Caring breeds joy.

Doing the right thing promotes joy. Reaching out promotes joy. There is always something to be done somewhere, for someone. You are needed. Being needed creates joy. Again, as long as the giving is not on the burdensome side.

Finishing something creates joy. Starting something new creates joy. More than once I have heard people say, "When I retire, I want to write! Oh, I have a story in me." Just start. There is no magic to looking for new work, losing weight, writing a novel, or any wish for that matter. It is just to start. The start creates joy.

Being kind to yourself promotes joy. Knowing at the end of the day, you did your best. Knowing the "best you" showed up for the day creates joy.

5

I am happy... I am happy...I am Happy

Gratefully, we can only think of one thing at a time. Right! So why not keep a great attitude, by making sure that the thoughts we are thinking are positive ones? Positive thoughts beget a positive attitude. How easy is this?

This is not very easy at all. We know our minds race in so many directions. We worry about things that may never happen. If they do happen, guess what, we handle the situation. Can we tell our minds this? At times, yes.

How do we keep our minds clear from negative thoughts? One way is to have a mental bag of tricks: affirmations, mantras, or prayers that we turn to in daily life, and in difficult times.

So what is an affirmation, a mantra or prayer? Again, from Webster's dictionary. An affirmation is a positive declaration, a mantra is a chant and prayer is a humble request. I don't know about the last definition on prayer. Sometimes I have not been so humble in my prayers. I have been brazen and begging at times.

Let me share with you one of my favorite sayings. During the expanding scope of my work, especially in the lean times, this is what I would say. "I am not to want, I am not to worry, I am not in a rush, I am not in a hurry." Let me break this saying down. The "not wanting" was to be grateful for whatever I had. The "not to worry" was to eliminate the worry to proceed moving forward. The "rush and hurry" was to know I needed to calm down so I could proceed in a more relaxed manner. I believe nothing done in anxiety is ever done well. Did this work for me? I think so.

There are many books of daily affirmations or prayers. You can start by creating your own or using someone else's. Start by always speaking positively and kindly to yourself. Say things in the present tense, because your future is created right now. Do not say I will be happy. I will be well. That speaks to tomorrow. Tomorrows are created presently. Replace with the present sayings. *I am happy. I am well.* We only have this moment in time, so treat it like this is it. This present creates your great tomorrows. Here's a start of some great sayings. You probably have many more that you can add.

I am Happy.

I am well.

I am calm.

I am getting better and better every day.

I am a winner.

I achieve.

I excel.

I am peaceful.

I am safe.

I am happy...

Get rid of any negative speaking, both internal and external. Sayings like "Oh, I am such a dummy!" Are you? Or "Boy, am I slow!" Are you? If you say these negative things about yourself, guess what! People will believe you. At the job when looking for a person who could be promoted, are the bosses going to promote "You, the slow dummy!" Not likely.

Try looking in the mirror, saying your phrase of choice. At times it may be hard to meet your own eyes. Who is that stranger that I may have been treating not so kindly? This may take a little time, but it will get easier as you get more confident.

Some people recommend having your positive saying posted everywhere. Read the sayings daily. Read them out loud on the way to work or school. Get these great thoughts into your psyche. Wear the thoughts like a pair of comfortable slippers. Keep in mind, this may be new to you and anything new takes time before it becomes comfortable.

Activity will also keep the mind clear of negative thoughts that create a negative attitude. If you are in the middle of a home project, you can't be thinking the negative thoughts. You have to pay attentions to the hammer, the paint, that hot glue gun or electric saw.

When you lose yourself in an activity, you lose the demons that chase you. Let me stop here and say I couldn't possibly name all the demons we could face in a lifetime: insecurity, jealousy, greed, hate, debt, illness, betrayal, grief. The list is endless and so personal.

If you are involved in an athletic activity, how can you think the negative thoughts when you have to concentrate on the ball coming at you, or the next turn on the bike, or the current pose in yoga? Exercise is really the magic pill for great health, a clear mind, a fabulous look and positive attitude. Those wonderful physical chemicals called endorphins are released during exercise. You become fit, you feel better, you act better.

When doing any type of exercise, you become a force to be reckoned with. You did it! You alone chose this aspect of yourself. No matter where your starting point is, there will always be something more that can be done. There is low-impact everything. An example of this is exercise done in water to lessen the strain on your joints. Very low-impact. There are so many options available price-wise and choice-wise. Always consult a physician, and ask for medical clearance before starting any new venture into exercise if you have never done it before.

Work also works. To lose yourself in a good day's work, greatly adds to good attitude. Whatever your issues may be health-wise, in relationships, or with yourself, good work can be a comfort. It can be a known entity that moves you forward through a challenging day.

One of the ways to keep positive is to pray your way through something. I may not know your God or what you may call your God, but for those who believe in one, you pray. For those who are atheists, skip this paragraph or chapter. Praying or saying a mantra, an affirmation or chanting will put you in an altered state of being. I am not saying put a pyramid on your head, and sit on a hilltop. This is private and this is personal and we all do this (again except the atheist with no prayer, but I bet they have their own mantras).

We ask please give me the strength to get through this day, please handle these atrocities that are on me. Please let me have a day that takes me that one step closer to recovery. Please grant me peace. Please don't let the dog eat my homework. Please find the solution, please provide a cure, an answer or a healing. Please grant a miracle.

Scientists say that prayer works. There are studies that say if you pray you will heal faster and if someone else is praying for you, you will heal faster. Is it that when we pray, we are calmer? A directed present moment without scattered thoughts creates calmness? It is a peacefulness that is not only relaxing, but lets healing in on all levels? I don't have any answer, but I have known it to work.

So let's begin, or continue, by saying.....

I am happy, I am happy, I am happy. I am safe, I am well, I am a success, I am at peace, I am special, I am happy.

6

Practice, Practice, Practice

Right this moment I have a very bad attitude towards having to write this book. I want to be doing anything else. Like an undisciplined child or should I say an undisciplined adult, I ask myself how I can leave my office and do anything but write today. I hear the cats fighting, the laundry calling, and maybe I should return a friend's email. I just don't want to do this. I am aware that if I do not sit and focus, and continue to write this book, it never will be completed. Plus the laundry can wait, the cats always stop fighting on their own and I can email my friend later.

What makes a person do what they do not want to do? Not promoting hours of nagging thoughts: "I should have done this or that"? This internal nagging and strife are drastically pulling any great attitude towards the bad side. What is it? It is the discipline of practice, and the knowledge that practice makes close to perfect. Nothing is ever perfect, but practice gets us close.

Consider your personal history of practice. Things that you are great at today took practice to get there. It took the time, effort and repetitive behavior to be as good as you are today in something. This could be as simple as riding a bike, or as frightening as public speaking. It takes practice to be comfortable with something. Practice to weave new behavior into the fabric of your life.

If you are by nature a negative person, or have spent your life surrounded by complainers and negative behavior, how will you be able to set out for that magically positive attitude? You practice, practice and practice. You practice till the practice becomes you.

When you are about to start something new for yourself, it starts with the first step or first thought. Let's say you want to be more positive on your job. You then say, "I will start with the practice of not saying one negative thing to anyone or myself for a half-hour today." You may have to set the gauge to your own barometer. Maybe start with 10 minutes. Then the next day do 15 minutes or a half-hour. You will feel the difference immediately. Watch the world around you change, because of your new attitude.

I am a firm believer to have the best attitude at work you dislike, start looking for new work. The moment you decide to make a switch will change your attitude. You will feel empowered to be looking to get out of your current situation. The movement forward will fuel you with the great thoughts that soon you will be resigning from your current place of employment, to go on to the next best opportunity for yourself. This changes one's attitude immediately.

We can go another level here. Let us now practice not taking in a negative person's "stuff" for 5 minutes, or 15 minutes, or ever. We know that being near a negative person is deadly to a great attitude. This is hard, but there are ways to keep the negative at bay at work or home. Get off the phone sooner. Walk out of a room faster. Negative people are everywhere, every day. Negative people can be co-workers, neighbors, a relative, a spouse. They even show up at church on Sunday. It is your choice how you handle them. We want to spend time with the great deal of wonderful people who are positive, rather than one moment with those who aren't.

Another good way to achieve a positive attitude in your life is to observe those who are positive. To build great attitude, look closer. How do they walk? How to they hold themselves? Now, you do it. I am not saying be a clone of another. What I am saying is walk your best walk of confidence. If you don't know what that looks like, look around you; see what others are doing. Now practice. Practice your own style.

The best time to practice this is when there is a long uninterrupted space to walk. Alone is best, so you do not have any distractions. If there are strangers all around and you start to feel foolish, who cares? They do not know you. Park your car the furthest away (and safely of course) to a mall entrance, or supermarket, or home repair store, any of those store complexes with huge parking lots. For those who live in the city without a car, go to a different neighborhood and try this. Your choice. For those of you who travel, practice walking the long distances in the airport terminals.

Ladies, bag over your shoulder, arms down. Gentlemen, hands out of the pockets and arms down. Now walk. Head up, shoulders back. You could imagine being called up on a stage for an award. What award? You choose.

The winner is called. That winner is you. You have to leave your seat and walk. You are not going to walk up for an award with shoulders bent or head down. You are going to shine your brightest.

Once you start practicing, a couple of things will happen. You will start feeling secure with yourself. You are being in the moment. Being in the moment puts a lot of demons on the shelf, so they are not currently bothering you. The more you practice feeling secure and proud in your walk, the more the world will treat you this way. You will become more positive. You do not have to say a thing. You are exhibiting a positive attitude. You will begin to walk like this daily, in shorter distances. You begin to walk your worth.

Practice smiling. Most days we plod along doing the daily routines and not smiling too much. Yet there is so much to be grateful for. Daily. So practice smiling. Smiling is so contagious! If you smile at someone, what happens? They usually smile back.

If you want the world on your side, here is the key. Keep smiling. The world will smile back. Smiling is a natural companion with having a great attitude. Practice with strangers. Choose a safe environment, of course. See the reaction of a smile versus a frown. I won't name names, but some of the "joy robbers" may not smile back. That is OK. You keep smiling.

Once you have observed another's stance and behavior, let us observe our own minds for behavior patterns. What we want to do is to start to think about what we want to be like. What type of work, home, relationship, health, or life we want to have.

How do you do this? By practicing visualization. I have mentioned this before in other books. It is too important not to mention again. What you mentally see is what you will or can be. It works. You see in your mind the life you want to lead, and practice thinking thoughts that will put you there. Visualization is seeing in your mind what you would like your world to look like.

See yourself in the best work environment. See yourself finishing that next project. See yourself handling that next interesting encounter with grace. See yourself handling difficult situations as they occur. See yourself walking on your own, without physical therapy or a cane. See yourself in a relationship of love and trust. Seeing myself with my third book in hand as I give a new workshop.

I have heard stories of people who visualize themselves in grand situations when their reality is anything but grand.

Ask any successful person about their thoughts. I am sure they would say they always think winning thoughts. Their thoughts drove them forward to success. So why not you?

What you think, is what you become. Along the way, also think of things we may need, or are nagging at us and must be attended too. I was thinking about how I should be handling a new computer program. I am not a driver. I don't like to drive; none of my friends ever ask me to drive. Ummm! I know this. What happens? I receive a flyer in the mail from a community college for a class on the computer program I'm interested in learning. The location is three miles from where I live, at one of their satellite locations. Not a drive I can't or won't do. The class was being held on a Saturday morning, causing no conflicts with my work time or travel time. It was clearer than clear. I must attend. I paid for the course, and received the information I needed.

If you pay attention to your mind, you will see the same happenstance's occur. By your watchful thinking, you create the synchronicity to your life. Your thinking can actually create your opportunity. If you visualize what you need or want, I assure you, you will start to see the way. Putting out the request comes back with a result. Sometimes even better than you thought of. This could also be called daydreaming big. So dream big.

Another technique to keeping positive is to practice reading one positive thing a day. You can do the simplest of reading: a daily calendar saying, to one page out of a book on positive thinking. Recently I was feeling "miffed." I recognized I was reading four daily readings a day, which were too much for me to absorb. Two were on my nightstand, one on my desk and another on the kitchen counter. One is fine, four is overload. You want to read the positive and have it sink in. Reading four felt like more responsibility and work, not the positive lift I was needing. If you do not have the privacy at home or at work to read these daily sayings, keep the information in your car, purse, bookbag, locker, whatever works for you.

Do watch what emotions you choose. Your chosen emotions produce your attitude. Practice choosing love in your heart, and not hate. This is not as easy as it sounds. When there is a person or situation that is so extreme, you may have just been too hurt or too attacked. It may take a long while to forgive the "attacker." Meanwhile, *get rid of any hate in your heart.*

Studies have shown if we stay positive, it will only benefit our health. If you can control the hateful thoughts, it truly cuts down on any illnesses you may incur. Symptoms of illness will be lessened. Is this easy? NEVER. If you stay in hateful thoughts, frowning, tightening of the stomach muscles, what is achieved? Wrinkles, an ulcer or worse.

Coming to this conclusion may take the assistance from an "expert," such as a therapist. I must stop here and mention the benefits of seeking outside help. We were not born automatically with the tools that it may take to practice overcoming obstacles in our lives. There are so many situations that can take a toll on us that may never have existed in history before. What is one to do? We must reach out and find assistance. Our goal is to get the best tools, to make our days the best they can be.

You can read everything on a subject, and attempt to apply it to your personal situation. That is fine. I feel that an outside therapist will scale down the time it takes to heal. You can heal alone or you can find a helping hand that will assist you to heal quicker. Why waste time in the drama of a painful situation? Why not get through the healing process sooner than later? Find the right therapist for you. Pick your life up again and begin anew.

If you are in a situation and do not have the tools to handle that situation, find the people who can help you. There are lots of agencies that provide assistance for nominal (or no) fees. The experts will be able to provide you with the helpful tools for you to practice.

Practice a behavior that becomes you. Look around you. What are others doing that you want to do? Practice that behavior. Nothing that takes effort is ever easy. Practice techniques that add to your life, not delete from it. Practice yourself right into that successful life you deserve. What happens when you achieve that practiced positive attitude, and your life becomes a better place to live in? You keep practicing and practicing and practicing to maintain your best life.

7

Be Good to Get Good

What we believe, we achieve. What we give, we receive. Every time you choose an action or thought, there is a reaction. This is the law of cause and effect. Knowing there is a reaction to every action keeps us in check. We all have witnessed worlds spin out of control when knowingly a wrong action was chosen, resulting in a firestorm of reaction.

Let's say we choose to say something nasty to someone. The reaction may be that the other person says a nasty comment back. They may tell others how awful we are. Other people may react by treating us in a nasty way. Knowingly saying something offensive will cause a domino effect of reactions. Is this the way you want to live your life?

Be cautious with the words you speak. They are powerful, with lasting qualities about them. The nature of our present words will determine our futures. And as the old saying goes, "If you can't say a nice thing about somebody, don't say anything at all." Easy? Hardly.

Another example of cause and effect is the reaction to stealing. I am not talking about bank robbing. I am talking about your stealing time. Do you steal time from your job? Not being where you're supposed to be, or heading out earlier than you should. Who does it hurt? Your employer? When you get caught, the seed of mistrust is planted. It may hurt you getting a good reference for your next job. Who did you steal from? Yourself! There are lots of levels of stealing: time, ideas, space or stealing things.

To keep the good in our lives daily, choose one small effort of doing good and see what happens. I read about a person who was picking up one piece of litter a day to do their part for "good." Just one piece of litter. I started to do it. It feels good. I don't pick up something that is not safe but a bottle, can or paper. Pick it up, throw it away. In the article, the person said when she did this she witnessed a stranger watching her. They did the same thing. This bit of good created a ripple effect. A litterless world perhaps. I hope so.

Keeping the feeling of good in your heart will promote good coming to you. This is that feeling you get when you do something nice. You may feel this way around the holidays by giving a little more to charity. This is a start. I think charity begins in the home. Who can you assist in your family, neighborhood or community? Branch out to do world charity work, after you handle the local. There are animal shelters, foodbanks, girls/boys clubs, and hospitals that need you. What is it that you feel strongly about? We are all different and feel comfortable in different settings. What do you like to do? You have skills to help others. This is all about generosity. The more you give, the more you will receive.

Serve when called upon. You may not have any answers in a particular situation, but if you are called upon to watch the kids, pets, the elderly, do it with a smile. The good we feel when we give, indeed assists us with the positive attitude we need to live our lives. Feeling good creates a good attitude. Simple.

Good manners create good cause and effect. Please and thank you's are powerful words. An appreciation of someone's work, be it an employee, co-workers, or the painter, is a must. Thank everyone who helps you! Everyone wants to be acknowledged for their work or a deed well done. In return, how you treat others will be how you are treated in kind.

Let's say you are in one of those horrid life situations. A horrid life situation could be a divorce, a legal dilemma, maybe a medical issue or anything that is a big problem to you. This problem is present daily and seems to have no resolution in sight. We do not know how long these "horrid situations" will last. Why sit in the stew and create more problems? You may be sacrificing your health or happiness.

Please give yourself a break. Reaching out with one phone call, letter, or email to provide you with the tools to conquer the present challenge, you are ahead. You cannot live in a "horrid situation" without it affecting you. You choose the level of how something can affect you. You choose to bring the good to you, or you choose to be miserable.

If you know you are handling this "horrid situation" to the best of your abilities, you win. You win, knowing you are doing your best, knowing you are responsible for your welfare.

There are so many things that can happen to us. We may never know the "why" of the circumstance at the time. Yet a number of times we can reflect, "Oh! I see why that was so hard."

The situation taught me...

I met during the situation…

I got involved with…

I got involved in... The list goes on…

The mystery of the rhyme and reason to life truly is fascinating.

No matter what your situation at this moment, know that it will change. Know that doing good for yourself, will get the good to yourself. Present that good attitude, to have the best reaction back to you.

So, be good to get good. You deserve this!

8

We build a life, not have a life

We choose our views, count our blessings, think the thoughts that entertain us, be those thoughts nightmarish or fabulous visualizations. These things all contribute to our present attitude. Now we must continue to choose the best, to maintain a good attitude. Remember we build a life, not have a life. We are the ones who are responsible to choose the attitudes that set the stages we walk on personally, professionally, spiritually and physically. Why not choose the best?

There are always different choices to make, at different times in our life, which affect the attitude we have. A simple example of this: some people choose to go to college in their twenties, and some choose to go to school to finish their degrees in their fifties. This is ours to build one's life for comfort and security, with the best-fit profession. If you are the best you, in your world, you know what will be best. This could be a GED for one or a PhD for another. The choice of timing is always ours. Do something now or later.

Some of us carry around that extra 20 pounds (or more) for years or decades, until it is just so uncomfortable we decide to make the commitment to lose weight.

Choosing a different lifestyle builds a new model of ourselves. "Gifting" ourselves a new look. Making a choice of a leaner body leads us towards keeping a healthier self. Some of us finally choose to quit smoking, adding to a healthier life.

Some people stay in unsettled marriages or relationships for years, or decades, until forced with a choice for a more peaceful lifestyle. We may choose to work at the relationship, or to leave the relationship.

Sometimes we choose to finally mend fences with others to dissolve a rift. Dissolving the rift will promote more inner peace and a better attitude. This resolve usually feels like a weight has been lifted off our shoulders. That lift clears the mind, to make room for that great visualization or pleasant thoughts. Mending bad feelings can be done without even involving the other person. This person could be living or dead. You mentally mend the fence, and go forward. This goes along with the old adage "forgive and forget." Not easy, but necessary for peace of mind.

When you make the choice to be the best you that is you, you create a belief that is you. A belief that you are, and will be working for, the best that is available. Some of your choice practices become life long. The amount of exercise or daily calories one needs to be fit keeps the weight down. This is not hit or miss. It is a life-long process.

Belief is also accepting challenges with grace, as well as a great attitude. To look at the dilemma, assess it, and proceed forward gracefully, you must first look at the history of your life. Recognize your own personal rhythms. Haven't you had situations in your life, that at one point looked like there were no solutions? Yet the situation came to a resolve. This is that, "When one door closes, another one opens" theory. Better a door than a high window, I say.

It may take years to make the choice of what needs attention. What needs to be handled, built, or rebuilt? Sadly, sometimes it takes years for us to "show up" in our lives. Showing up means taking the responsibility for the life you want to live. Don't like your current life? Take responsibility to build a new one.

I have witnessed this showing up and taking responsibility first hand. It transforms someone into the person they deserve to be. Just by them taking charge of their life. It is the tiniest of steps that beget the greatest changes. The simplest two-letter word NO can release the flow of great change in oneself.

No, I no longer will do.

No, I no longer will be.

No, I no longer will have.

No, I am not available.

There are times the choice of change is made for us. A health scare to lose the weight. A spouse asking for a divorce, or to be suddenly widowed. A job loss that put a strain on any spending. This strain then gives a person the discipline to live a more frugal lifestyle, to gain financial control over your money. Maybe a new discipline added, to save and get out of debt.

At this time in history, the world is just filled with choices that never existed with such flexibility before.

We don't have to choose a 9 to 5 job. There are many flexible working options available. We can even mix it up: work out of our homes, travel for work or work in an office. We can mix up the times we go to these locations.

Personally, we can choose to raise a family or not. Marry or not. There are options of personal lifestyles today: alone, as a couple, as a part of a group.

It is interesting as we grow and stretch in this well-lived life. There are never-ending great surprises, and sometime heartaches. If your attitude is in the "right" frame of mind, the heartache is a bit easier to handle and the hurt does not last as long. The best-built life has added many coping skills to get through the hard times, those tools mentioned earlier.

No one walks this life without being "called up" to handle something of a challenging nature. This can take the form of family tragedies, or personal tragedies. Your belief must be knowing you will handle what is given. Also believe that in time, you will be centered again. You may live just a little differently, but centered and peaceful. You will look for the best solutions to living with the challenge that has presented itself.

I have come to realize the hardest times I've had, made me find more coping skills to keep my world balanced. Some of these skills I added are such a blessing now. I never would have tried some of the things I have, if not for the hard times. Reaching out to become more peaceful. These coping skills are personal and individual. They may include a new hobby, new types of exercise, better friendships, more play, more faith, more time alone, more time with people you love. The list is endless, and so is the building.

What limits us to building a great life with a great attitude? One thing is "limiting beliefs." Learning is process. This learning starts at birth. How you were raised, what you took in as a child. After you leave the parental world, and go out to work or go to school, we see there are different ways to live. There comes a time when the choice is yours. How do you want to live your life?

We are always building our lives with our choices. What will be the best choice for ourselves?

Let's get the hammers out, and start the building today. The best lived life for ourselves needs the best attitude. It is always our choice.

9

Caring for Yourself

If you're still young, you're lucky. If you're older, you're in the majority of just getting this next concept. Regardless, by a certain age we understand the saying, "If I don't take care of myself, no one else will." How often have we heard this saying? Yet when does it sink in?

I think it sinks in, when one realizes the prince/princess is not coming to rescue you, your lottery numbers weren't picked and exercise is the magic pill for the best health and weight loss. The bottom line is, this life is yours only. Your life is all about taking the best care of yourself! Keeping yourself at your best, so you can give your best to the rest of the world.

I love the word "honor." It is so regal-sounding and used to describe a pact or a promise. Honor is to have regard or respect. How do we honor ourselves? Do we respect ourselves? Do we have regard for ourselves? Do we treat ourselves in a special way? I am not saying being conceited and forgetting all responsibilities of work or family or both. I am talking about keeping ourselves out of harm's way, in all areas of our lives.

In relationships, if there are physical and verbal abuses we will not stand for either. Are you surrounded by people to whom you are invisible? People you don't fit with? Not because of religious or racial differences; you just don't fit. These are not your people. They may look exactly like you, but you just don't mix well with them. Stay with people who see you, enjoy you, and want to be with you.

Let's examine the work place. Now, I have been invisible there. I've raised my hand in the meeting, given a solution to a problem, and not been recognized. Then the next person gives the same solution. Wow, they get credit. That is when you know you have to start to look for new work.

Are you employed at work that you love? If not, are you doing the kind of work that is temporary and getting you through until school is finished, the kids are grown, out of college or until you retire? Knowing why we work: is it for the money? The fame? The personal satisfaction and socialization? It is this awareness that will keep us centered. The awareness of why we do something helps us to maintain a great attitude.

To dislike what you do for a living, is a disservice to yourself. It is a disservice to the children that you may be raising. If they hear that work is so hard and not a good place to be, they most likely will mirror your image and enter into an unsatisfying work life for themselves. They will believe that work is bad and hard. We know that great work makes a person's spirit soar with confidence and independence! Great work empowers the soul. Let me add, however, even with great work, time off is a must to regroup.

We all have choices. If the work is not great, then get yourself into a program that will assist you to find the work that is best for you. Go back to school. Get a degree. If not a degree, fulfill the requirements for a certification that says you passed something. Volunteer at something you think you might like, to see if it fits you. Yes, this may take some time scheduling. And yes, this scheduling may be a bit uncomfortable for a short time. This is what caring for yourself is, to do things now to build your future of new beginnings. This caring for yourself is an honoring wisdom.

Spiritually, do you find the time and places to speak to and be with your God? The time may be your personal Sabbath, or daily in your home. How we will keep up the "bathing" in our personal faith is honoring ourselves. Faith assists us with having a great attitude.

When we honor ourselves, we take the best daily care of ourselves. Yes, the 20 pounds will come off in time. In the meantime, we watch our food intake and put on the sneakers and go out for a walk. Do something that will keep you moving a couple of times a week. This does not take money. It takes time. We all have the same hours in the week. It is how we handle that time that will also keep our great attitude. If it means you have to get up a little early to get that jog or walk in, so be it. The benefits far outweigh the inconvenience. You are caring for yourself.

We must care for ourselves even more so, when we are faced with bothersome people. My friends and I will talk about being with people who leave a residue after you are with them. This residue is the toxic emotions that last for hours, sometimes days, after an encounter. It's hard to shake off their negative vibes. This could be in any situation: a workplace, a home life, or chance encounter.

It doesn't matter where this happens. Know that there will always be situations, for as long as we live, that will come with that residue. Once we recognize that a possible situation is going to happen, or just happened, we are better able to handle it. Let's say a family function or company outing is on the calendar. It's not your choice of spending time, but you have to go. Once recognized, this may be a problem, but the residue does not last that long. You know by carrying around any toxic feelings it is only hurting yourself. We may have those feelings, recognize them, but we don't let them last too long.

A "good attitude" way to look at a possible dreadful situation coming up is to put a time limit on the event. Let's say it's a wedding, and your not-so-pleasant ex will be there. Or a corporate event, where your old boss who demoted you will be there. Put a time limit on it. Say to yourself, "I only have to be at this event five hours. What is five hours in my lifetime?" Not much. It tricks you into being calmer and thinking "I can handle this." A friend does this around the holidays. He will say, "I only have to spend six hours a year with these people. After the six hours, I can leave and return home to my safe haven for holiday cheer." This time limit technique will cut down on the residue of toxic feelings.

Caring for yourself is recognizing the good you do for yourself when you take the first step at anything that honors you. Give yourself that great applause that you sidestepped the joy robber, got off the phone sooner, or walked away quicker from the energy drainer.

Caring for yourself is giving yourself credit. You are working on that next new employment, new great project or new positive behavior. Be proud of yourself for any bit of good you do for you.

Another technique to keep and maintain a great attitude is to recognize and observe emotions. Some therapists say to "check in" every couple of hours. Do a body check. Checking your body for emotions.

Are you feeling tense? Where is the tension? Do you have a headache, stomachache, or any pain?

Whatever feelings you have, will affect your attitude. It is best to take a closer look at them. This could be as simple as getting a headache, a possible alert sign to slow down or a signal to a more serious illness. Watch when you are hitting into things, breaking and dropping things. Is it time to take a rest? Take a break? Stop rushing? Stop living on autopilot? Remember, stress kills. As long as you are doing something that is for the better, it will alleviate the stress. If you keep your body under a lot of stress, the body will break. Sometimes we are able to heal and recover, but if given enough stress, the body will start to break and may not recover. Which do you choose?

On the other side of the coin, recognize what does it feel like to feel great, no pain, or headaches or stress? Keep a memory of those feelings. Start to recognize, hold on to what feeling great feels like. What does it feel like to look into the eyes of a loved one? Do you feel loved and safe and happiness? Look in the eyes of your pets. Same feelings. Recognize them; hold on to these feelings. Keep them in the reserve, to use as a visualization to calm you.

Feel the hand of a child that reaches for ours. Such love and trust. To honor oneself is to surround oneself with this love. To only enter in relationships of love. Now we know this is not possible in all daily living, but keep those feelings tucked in our hearts to guide us through the struggles of the day.

During times of high stress, we need to dig deeper for more coping skills. We were not born with these skills to care for ourselves; they are learned. Remember, whatever you are going through at the present, means something for later. The situation is preparing you for something later. What that is, you don't know.

I have had some pretty odd times. Struggle times. We all have. Later you looked at what brought you to a new way of living. You are forced to live a different level of your life and it proves to be better. A place where maybe you don't accept certain bad behavior any longer. Don't accept less than the best for yourself. This means in all areas of your life.

We no longer accept bad behavior from others. If it is at work with a cruel boss, it may be time to go or look within the company for a new position. Always remember you have choice. Does the position of staying outweigh the bad treatment? Your choice.

Do not condone bad behavior with your services. Why is it some of us will condone bad service behavior! Condoning bad behavior just keeps that bad behavior going. Stop going to, or shopping at, any company or single proprietor that does not respect you. It is always your choice what level of service is your personal acceptance level.

To care for oneself is to keep us centered as best we can. We don't have to answer every phone call, or every email. Right away, or ever at all. Also, mind your own business. What a great phrase. This phrase could be said to someone else. Or to yourself: "Mind your own business." Stay in your own life.

I am sure we all have some family member that is "talked about." Everyone has an opinion on so-and-so. After decades of this chatter, you have got to think, "How boring is this!" If you want to be left alone with your business, leave other people alone. Do I practice this all the time? I can get caught up with the best of them in gossip and hearsay. As I get older, I just find this wasteful energy, but do I still listen? Yeah, I am human.

To keep a great attitude is to treat yourself special. What does that mean to you? Schedule special time; yes, schedule it, or it will never get done. When are your mental health days? Play a fun thing alone, or with someone. This does not take money, but it does take a structure of your time.

Do you only rest when you get that backache or that headache? Rest is for us to give to ourselves so we do not put our body in a constant alert mode.

Something to look forward to gives us joy and shows that we care for ourselves. Also, why haven't you signed up for that painting, yoga, Chinese cooking or fly-fishing course? You deserve it!

Remember, there will always be an unlimited list of distractions, obligations, and responsibilities that take up our time. It is for our best attitude that we sort through the list to see which are real and don't fit us any longer. I work out of my home. I do receive the early morning calls while I am in the midst of writing. My choice is to answer the call or not. No writing, no book. Easy choice.

Yet there are levels of boundaries setting that are just so hard. You do have a choice to get involved with the distractions or to let it go. Your choice may waffle, when those desperation calls from family or friends come in. You want to help. Remember, the resolve will come in either way without any input of yours. This really goes for most "drama." You have a choice of the amount of time you want to listen, or can listen. Support someone to the level that you can accept, for your own peace.

Sometimes we are put into situations that we just don't understand. This could be an unexpected lawsuit or accident, layoff, divorce, and we want our "OLD" life back. This is a big attitude adjustment time. Those times are when we must dig deep, and find our place of peace. Stay with the people who love us. Fuel ourselves with all that is good. Count our blessings daily. While in the middle of the firestorm, you can't see it, but you can believe it. All storms stop. No one situation goes on forever. Situations change. What does happen in time? Everything works out. It always does.

If you can't change the situation, change the attitude toward the situation. I know people who are so anguished about things that are not in the present. What will happen when my child starts school? Meanwhile the child is in diapers. Some people have fears about if they have to move when they retire. They may have years to make that move, or till retirement. They keep themselves on a high level of anxiety. This high level of anxiety only will give you more wrinkles, and maybe an ulcer. Put these changes "on the shelf." I will look at this in five years, a year before I retire, or have to move. Remember life is constantly changing, and all our situations change in surprising ways. So why waste the time in worry?

Meanwhile, join the company bowling league or local garden club. Both things will continue in your future visualized life. Don't waste the present in dread of the unknown future. We don't know what the future holds. Why sit in worry?

Taking care of yourself is gathering the tools to provide yourself with the best life. Some of those tools we covered in this book: recognizing you hold the view of your world, choosing your view is choosing your attitude. Being grateful for where you are at the moment as the moments flow and change. Centering our thoughts daily for our direction. Choosing good and taking the pen to paper, the brush to canvas, the thought to speech to build your life. All items that we have control over. All attitude is your choice.

Gift yourself your best day. What would that day look like? How are you caring for yourself? Gift yourself the best days for your best life.

Choose your best. It's your *ATTITUDE!*

About the Author

Karen Okulicz is the author of "Try! A Survival Guide to Unemployment" and "Decide! How to make any Decision."

Both books are resources utilized with workforce development programs. They have an honored placement on the Self-Publishers Hall of Fame. Foreign rights have been sold to Mexico, Japan, Indonesia, Russia and Korea.

Ms. Okulicz is a continued invited speaker to national conferences on career and workplace issues. She has hosted and produced the radio show "Workline."

She continues to maintain her best attitude at the Jersey shore.